Roberts' *Pigtown* is part love letter and part battle cry. His poetry explodes off the page with an unflinching fury wrapped in a deep desire to reach for the light through the darkness and to speak for the silent. He weaves a poetic tale of struggle, loss, triumph, and survival on the gritty streets of Baltimore.

Pigtown is relentless and gripping, much like the city that inspired it.

—Shannon Haire, author of *Patriots, Petticoats, and Partition*

PIGTOWN

Anthony Roberts

PIGTOWN
Copyright © 2017 Anthony Roberts

ISBN-13: 978-1-970003-15-4

Cover artwork/photography © 2017 Blue Kevra
www.cautionblue.com
Biography Picture © 2017 Property of Red Dashboard LLC/WAMPP

Independently edited by Rita Anderson

Published by
Red Dashboard LLC Publishing
Princeton NJ 08540
www.reddashboard.com

For the four most beautiful poems still being written,
Elizabeth, Gianna, Alex, and Tristan

Table of Contents

Introduction 3

Shut Up! 4

Introit 7

Pigtown 8

History in Eighths 33

HIVe Mind, 1986 37

Baltimore Fragment 39

The Buttery Restaurant Baltimore, 1990 41

Nocturnal Thoughts 44

Author's Biography
Subscript Notes

I'm so Baltimore I can get anywhere on two buses and one transfer; Old Bay has the same effect on me as Spice in Dune; I yell "Back Door!" on airplanes to see who gets it; I know John Waters has the best mustache; I know I would NEVER eat at Phillips; a Hammerjacks bumper sticker was the sign of a well-traveled individual; when you say Ripken, you're talking about Cal Jr.; Captain Chesapeake had never been on a real boat in his life; the News American was a better paper than the Sun; City Paper was better than either, and Al Sanders and Jerry Turner were the greatest newscasters ever.

Shut Up!

The voice boomed through two doorways and three rooms to reach me in my crib. That's where it began, my urge to be heard. I blame my father for many things, but the world can hold him responsible for the fact that I won't shut up.

I don't know what I said that bothered him so much. I was two and a half, maybe three, and my world was defined by whatever walls surrounded me at the time. More than likely, I was describing the things around me as I saw them and my father, trying to either sleep, cure a hangover, or just enjoy quiet, didn't care for my observations.

My Dad was yelling at me in my crib to shut up. Outside it was 1976, America was dying, but we didn't know it yet. The small piece of the world I inhabited in Southwest Baltimore would become simply another part of the body consumed by the dual assault of crony capitalist tumors and the inevitable death spiral of all empires.

Hard working people moved about outside of my awareness up their marble steps into their own row houses a decade away from the discovery of crack. Hard working fathers would become hollow eyed drunks and addicts who avoided their children at all costs. Dutiful housewives would become women abandoned, who welcomed any man who brought a moment's relief from the grind of loneliness and poverty.

4

I am getting ahead of myself. I'm still in my crib having just learned my first lesson:

Keep screaming no matter how much someone tries to silence you.

And the second lesson:

People want to hurt you, and the closer they are, the more they want to do it.
Had I known how to write, I probably would have started writing poetry in my crib.

6

Introit[1]

In the neighborhood
there was a factory: huge
it made boxes
Four stories
red brick
windows open in summer
the sound of machines
It made boxes
you could hear them
chop cut press hiss
chop cut press hiss
chop cut press hiss
chop cut press hiss
the crank and whir of progress

Then silence
a break
so sudden
your ears hurt

Lunch
the sound of machines replaced by bells
the tolling of the Angelus
a call to prayer
that no one says anymore
(except me sometimes)

Mournful
as if the bells themselves know
they will go unheard
unheeded
and not understood
I watch the workers in the morning
mostly women lining up
hoarse dry rasps of greeting
They sit and smoke
already old and worn tired
thighs degenerated
into forlorn forgotten ecstasies

The bell tolls
light a cigarette
inhale
Hail Mary, Full of Grace...

PIGTOWN[2]

I.

It was an easy place to remain
finish high school (or not)
get a job (or not)
get married (or not)
have kids (a certainty)
split up
find someone else
have more kids
surnames become clans
and franchised polygamy
without the vocabulary

Few ever dreamed
a trip to the ocean
was an adventure
a trip to a suburban mall
meant find preppy kids
and fight them
no one went to a museum
unless it was a field trip

the library (lieberry)
was only for school

Wine tastings were frequent
Mad Dog 20/20
Thunderbird
Bartles and Jaymes
Boone's Farm
Bucolic becomes blue collar

Trapped
the #11 bus was liberation
always condemned to return
until one day
I left
now when I return
it's as if I was never there

9

In January of 2015, after my best, but again futile attempt at self-destruction, I went back home. It had been almost two decades since I had been there for longer than a day or two. The city I grew up in was now strange to me. Old landmarks gone, replaced by buildings I didn't recognize, billboards advertising places I had never heard of, old haunts and hangouts now, replaced by signs and people as foreign to me as the Indies were to Columbus. The neighborhood though, was the same. The same sense of despair hung in the air. Young men hanging on corners with no place else to go. Corner stores still had entryways and security systems worthy of the US Embassy in Kabul. Prostitutes plying their trade on corners and front steps. Luxury cars parked in front of dilapidated row homes. A lone beat up and dented police car still drove languidly around less concerned with preventing crime and more concerned with containing it.

II.

A place makes you what you are
Shapes you
Pigtown made me

Street smarts learned from nights on corners
what it feels like to be sucker punched
hit with a skateboard
jumped when outnumbered
how a bat can be dodged
a knife can be hidden

Your hair stands up when you're being followed
Count the shadows behind you
watch their length
like malevolent mimes

I carried resentment
a chip on my shoulder
fuck your social work degree do-gooder
carried that for a long time-
still do to some extent

Judge me by my looks
on where I am from
on what I have
you will lose

I've wanted to fight you
for as long as I can remember
ever since the first time
I was laughed at for being poor

I win because
I want it more than you
I want to see you beaten
I will always have something to prove

A conference room
a bar
a classroom
a battlefield
it's all a street corner
and I am more comfortable here than you

13

Now back in the neighborhood, a stranger on the streets I once roamed, as foreign as a tourist from Iowa who had gotten lost looking for the Inner Harbor. The house where I grew up, torn down, a vacant lot they had attempted to turn into a community garden now resembles a cemetery. As a teenager, I spent as little time here as possible, seeking out the culture in other parts of the city this neighborhood lacked.

I stopped in the middle of Scott Street, next to the spot where I had stolen my first car stereo from a Pontiac Fiero. The corner of Hamburg where I kissed my first girlfriend. I stood in the middle of Sterrett Street, the locals giving me strange looks as I remembered the night I'd been jumped, learning what brass knuckles and a skateboard to the back of the head felt like. All within ten seconds of each other. Four of those guys were dead now, and the fifth will die in prison. I feel no pity.

III.

In Memoriam
Brad (stabbed)
Lori (AIDS)
Jimmy (stabbed)
Shaun (heroin)
Richie (heroin)
Molly (heroin)
Larry (hanged)
Brian (heroin)
Charlie (heroin)
Ollie (heroin)
Steve (shotgun to the face)
Lamont (pistol shot to the head)
Pat (AIDS or heroin, no one's sure which)
Billy (AIDS from Pat)
Wade (hanged)

Someone's statistics

they're DEAD
you're NOT

see the difference

It was the summer of 1987. The crack war was underway. Steve had been shot in the face, somewhere in Murphy Homes, and dumped in an alley two blocks away. His body wasn't discovered for three weeks.

The smell, another story.

Steve was only five feet and four inches tall. The neighbors said they thought his body was that of a dog. They didn't call the police, they called animal control. The poor civil servant knew something was up, because dogs don't wear Air Jordans.

At least they let him keep his shoes.

IV.

The fugitives
the refugees
the lucky ones
the selfish ones
call us what you like

Some made it out of the cave

Remembering Plato
the allegory that meant nothing in 6th grade
makes sense now
we saw the thing and not the shadow

We went back
we told our story
of the world outside the cave
and no one believed us

V.

There are still those who remain.
Do you remember them?
Do they remember us?

Facebook had jumped the shark and truly gone global when people from the neighborhood started friending me. Some still spelled phonetically, that is, F-O-N-E-T-I-K-L-E-E.

VI.

It was a summer of cicadas, remember?
Hot humid
the smells more pronounced as a result
garbage smells like a corpse
when left outside in the sun

Maggots squirm
a gleeful copulation with decay
feral animals lay panting in the heat
it's too hot
for even animals to fight

Window fans push hot air around
spreading the odor into living rooms
children outside splash in a fire hydrant
a break from heat and filth

The torrent of water
splashing, playing
the closest to a river or pool
that they will get

A few years prior
a child died
pushed in front of a car
by the hydrant's force

They built a wading pool
a concrete divot
named it after the child
the next summer
there was no funding
It's still empty

The firetruck arrives
a pipe-wrench
and the river runs dry
heat humidity and stench return
Mother-fucker

The sun sets
bringing a five-degree respite
the cave dwellers come out sit on stoops
hoping to catch a breeze

22

I remember green. The color I painted my face as a child, the desire to emulate commandos and soldiers while my friends pretended they were sports' heroes. The various hues in the woods, (they weren't really woods, just a small patch of trees and brush in the area near the railroad tracks), where I would go to hide. I would cover myself with the leaves. I would hide, while the teenagers made out and the stoners would huff glue and spray-paint in the center of a copse of vegetation. I had no idea what druids were then, some ancient ancestral memory followed my bones from Antrim, but that's what they were—Priests and Priestesses of self-destruction. The world that would cost brain cells was far more preferable to the one that we lived in. Chemical euphoria as the 11:46 Chessie Red Line shook the trees, moving boxcars and flatcars on to wherever; while we remained in the neighborhood. The caboose at the end of the train was green; it provided the illusion of escape.

VII.

Teen boys on corners—
boom boxes blaring,
long hair brushed and feathered,
tight jeans, Goody combs,
Metal band black t-shirts,
to own a car is to be king.

Teen girls in neon—
teased hair, eye liner
tanned legs, stacked socks
sit in groups.
To be in a car with a guy,
is to be queen.

An urban mating ritual
people age fast here

Children run through the alleys at night
playing games,
and hunting
rats—cockroaches—beetles
looking to stage fights between species.

My girlfriend was grounded—
confined to her room
we'd write each other notes
attached to a string.

Brief conversations stolen
when her parents would let her out
for a trip to the ice cream truck.

The Capulets and Montagues
would have admired our moxy.

VIII.

The first time
was a tragedy, a comedy
where neither of us knew our lines
only that it was expected
that we were supposed to fuck,
and in some way
we'd be different when it was done
and at least I was.
I don't know about her
and I'll be damned
if I can remember her name,
how sad is that?

The experience for which lovers dare
the poets declare the holy grail
the theologians debated
the moralists and hypocrites condemned
the artists glorified
reduced to writhing
as she pinned me down

An epileptic earthworm on a weight bench
while Led Zeppelin played in the background
embarrassed for no reason
Don't call me
I won't call you.

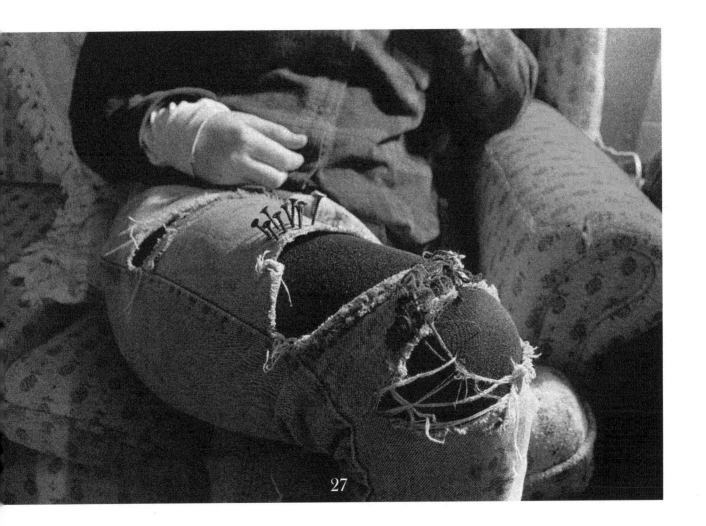

28

IX.

Have you ever been so hungry that
you've eaten donuts from a dumpster?
To this day I hate-

American cheese
Kool Aid
Ramen Noodles
Spaghetti O's
anything Chef Boyardee
the smell of Coors

I can go days without eating,
but my children never will.

Have you ever had to steal?
You feel more guilt
about filling your belly,
than Adam in the garden.
But sisters will sleep at night
without painful stomachs

So you do it again

X.

He destroyed the faith of many.
The priest they welcomed on a Palm Sunday
a wolf in shepherds' clothing,
It's a wonder I'm still Catholic

I had a friend
I used to resent him
he got special treatment.
We were all victims
some more than others.

Now I know
what that treatment was
"....", I am so sorry
I wish we had known
what to say
what to do
would anyone have believed us?

They say if you don't forgive,
you go to hell

I won't forgive

If I go to hell
I hope to see him there
I can spend eternity
beating the shit out of him
and I'll no longer have to ask for forgiveness

I went to my old church, it has a different name now. The memories within it just as strong—my Grandfather bringing me to mass as a child. My first Mass as an altar boy. The basement where our teen group had its haunted house, and I made out with a girl named Carrie. The room where Sid would play drums and I would play guitar. The good priests who saw something in me worth trying to save. The bad memories. My Grandfather's coffin being rolled up the aisle to a waiting hearse on a rainy Monday in September. The humiliation of being thrown out of church because I chose to wear a Mohawk and not dress according to someone else's expectation. The predator priest who used his position of trust to make Sundays a day I still hate. It all took a while to process.

I got into my car, and headed north. I was still a few hours from home. I thought about my kids, they'd be asleep when I arrived. Maybe I'd wake them and play some Clancy Brothers or read some Joyce. I kept driving. I didn't look back, I didn't need to. The neighborhood was in the car with me.

32

History in Eighths

The first poem was not my own
the words of a long-dead Irishman
who I used to seduce a mulatto girl
in the dark corner of an alley where bums pissed
when I kissed her she tasted of futility

The second poem was

Sound and color

as the acid

      dissolved

on my tongue

    my sweat (history on my skin)

a red-haired girl
talked me
down
when I kissed her she tasted like thunder

The third poem was one of
rhythm—form—structure
the most I've ever known
swirls of green black and brown
I created a muse of cadence cunning and violence
when I kissed her she turned her head and smiled

The fourth poem was one of despair
wrapped in malt hops and grape
all the while Sirens took pity
welcoming me
a hydra of forgotten names and accusations
when I kissed her she tasted like remorse

The fifth poem was one of fear
swaddled in a bundle.
The promises I made
     you will not be like me,
     you will not know want
my own eyes
staring back at me in a delivery room
when I kissed her she smelled of redemption

The sixth poem was one of destruction
I wrote with steel copper and C-4
and a voice that brought down fire
a child with henna hair and olive skin
walked with me through my Inferno
when I kissed her head
she smelled of cordite and gunpowder

The seventh poem was one of frustration
words became self-inflicted wounds
Munnin, perched on a witch's shoulder,
mocked me as I walked away
sounding the raven's cry of why
when I kissed her feathered crown
she tasted of regret

The eighth poem is one of wonder
contemplating an hour glass
a sagging breast
a whiskey bottle
struggling to understand how
they grew empty
when I kiss the breast
it tastes like memory

HIVe Mind 1986

When AIDS came onto the scene
it was a boon for boys entering puberty

Gone were the trips into bar bathrooms
to put quarters into the machine
promised ticklers and tantalizers
while Steve and Rob were lookouts
(they ran at the first sign of an adult)

Condoms became as common as baseball cards
trading Trojans and Jim Trahey held equal allure
Ty Cobb leering at tied up Bettie Page
in heated dreams of humid Baltimore summer

How many died so that we could see condoms
without furtive over the shoulder glances

Gay men suffered in silence
while the straight boys, testosterone filled, floundered and flustered
trying to roll round latex down
and found it was upside down
the biggest vocabulary word we knew was Nonoxynol-9

The drug users started to waste away
with tiny viral death sentences streaming
through hollowed tunnels into unsuspecting veins
maybe then we tasted fear
but Mountain Dew and Boone's Farm
drowned out the taste of everything else

    invincible
    immortal
    immoral
    ignorant

we made our way into the world
certain in the security
that only bad people died of the HIVe
we weren't bad
we just wanted to get laid

Baltimore Fragment

When was the last time someone in Baltimore wrote words worth remembering other than John Waters scribbling his number on a cocktail napkin 443-###-####?

In southwest Baltimore, the graffiti of Jam One and The Welfare Crew tagged all over a childhood of the 80s and 90s painted over in the name of gentrification by the hipsters who want the grittiness of city life but not the infection that comes with the dirt

What words are there? Carved into Poe's obelisk are a few, but the important ones were his last ones— the words no one heard him say, "I don't want to die here."

The Buttery Restaurant Baltimore, 1990

Sitting with a Lithuanian girl who reveals with every word
that her mind is not up to the task of the date
I make the mistake of giving her poems to read
which she is able to absorb for all of the time it takes
French fries to go from fryer basket to plate to counter to table
"It's nice but it doesn't rhyme."

It didn't rhyme, that would come later, life then more akin to a car collision or plane crash, hard conso-
nants meeting and twisting together trying to make sense of the chaos that, in the end, was random

That poem was
Birth, life, loss, learning, loss, the other, learning, learning, loss, faith filling the potholes and cuts of city
life

Later learning, leaving, basic training, shooting, stabbing, cutting, maiming, jumping, drinking, humping,
drinking, jumping, humping, drinking

* * *

And the rhyme begins
War, wife, life
daughter, daughter, son, slaughter, son
martyr to god of necessity
and now you see, dear lady,
after all this time
the poem finally rhymes

48

Nocturnal Thoughts

Watching my children sleep
I write from a place of certainty
where you haven't yet ventured
youth no matter how painfully lived
is expressed always in question marks or ellipses

I write from the tangled undergrowth
of desolate middle age
where the verdant woods of childhood
are seen for what they are
the stand of scrub pine
behind a vacant factory
every window broken
walls covered in graffiti
the overhead door rusted frozen half open
forever defying gravity
unable to descend
and find closure

I stand barefoot in a field
behind the factory
feet bleeding from 10,000 shards
that were once a stained glass window
the image of Mary holding the crucified
Christ

I understand her tears better now
imagine she's holding me
crucified by my own iniquities
each squandered heartbeat pushing blood through a body
driven by a mind convinced of immortality

I watch the children playing among the trees
oblivious to me
I am too old to be noticed in the world the young create
I have no place there
so I cannot exist
there is no room for cynicism
in a mind that makes redwoods of pine trees

I write from a place of certainty
I pray you may never find
may you never learn why
the aged seek solitude
it is not because I desire to be alone
I just don't want you to ever have anything
in common with me

Anthony Roberts is a veteran of Baltimore and Afghanistan. He is an Adjunct Professor of Writing at Fairleigh Dickinson University where he is also on the staff of *The Literary Review*. He is a graduate of The New School in New York City with a Master of Fine Arts degree in creative writing. His poetry has appeared in *The Other Voices Literary Anthology, Southerly Literary Journal*, and has been translated in Czech, Persian, Bengali, Hebrew, and Italian

He presently resides in Alexandria, NJ. In a home with beautiful views and interlocking fields of fire.

Subscript Notes:

[1] The psalm sung when the Priest approaches the altar for the Eucharist during the Roman Catholic Mass.

[2] Pigtown is a neighborhood in Southwest Baltimore, so named because pigs were herded from the train station at Camden Yards down the main street, Columbia Ave. (now Washington Blvd.) to the slaughterhouse off of Carey St, in the late 19th and early 20th centuries.

[3] Jam One and the Welfare Crew —A group of graffiti artists whose tags could be found throughout South and Southwest Baltimore.

93000500R00035

Made in the USA
Columbia, SC
07 April 2018